He Said She Said

Heidi-Lee Stockenström

DORRANCE
PUBLISHING CO
EST. 1920
PITTSBURGH, PENNSYLVANIA 15238

Dorrance Publishing Co
585 Alpha Drive
Suite 103
Pittsburgh, PA 15238
Visit our website at *www.dorrancebookstore.com*

ISBN: 978-1-6442-6663-2
eISBN: 978-1-6442-6681-6

For Jase, eternally grateful
and
Adam, I miss you

Winning the right to vote 100 years ago women hoped it would bring equity at last. However the fact that women hold fewer positions of power than men in politics and business the world we live in is still shaped very much from a males perspective. Are we entering a new time of transition that the suffragettes would have been proud of, the determination to eradicate the inequality and abuse of women the world over

The battle of the sexes – an age old dispute between men and women came to a head in 2017 with the international conversation about sexual misconduct taking centre stage. Accusations of sexual abuse and harassment by powerful men in the entertainment, political and other spheres led to the advent of the 'Me Too' and 'Time is up' movements. The reality of the abuse of power is startling. Although this constructive fury has resulted in a resolute pursuit of equity, the puritan persecution of men may have gone too far and fueled a hatred of men.

Accepting men and women are different psychologically and physically, these differences should be complimentary and form part of the richness and design of humanity. There are positive masculine and feminine traits and behaviors that should be encouraged in all individuals. This attitude may help us become a society in which there is less discrimination and greater equality for everyone.

As quoted by Emma Watson "Both men and women should feel free to be sensitive. Both men and women should feel free to be strong … it is time that we all perceive gender on a spectrum and not as two opposing sets of ideas."

'He Said She Said' shares quotes from men and women, including politicians, actors, philosophers, singers, authors and more. It explores the relationship between the sexes in an effort to bring them together through a series of thought provoking creative, humorous paintings.

Shared with a smile and desire to spread love and joy in our troubled world.

"What a woman wants is a reaction. What a man wants is a woman"

Charles Bukowski

"And when a woman's will is as strong as a man's who wants to govern her,
half her strength must be concealment"

George Elliot

"No one will ever win the battle of the sexes.
There's too much fraternizing with the enemy"

Henry Kissinger

"Ah, woman. They make the highs higher and the lows more frequent"

Fredich Nictzche

"I don't know why a woman would want any of the things men have
when one of the things that women have is men"

Coco Chanel

"If I had observed all the rules, I'd never have got anywhere"

Marilyn Monroe

"In politics, if you want anything said, ask a man.
If you want anything done, ask a woman"

Margret Thatcher

"Men and women, women and men. It will never work"

Erica Jong

"I don't even wait. And if you are a star, then they let you do it. You can do anything ... grab them by the pussy"

Donald Trump

"Woman are wiser than men because they know less and understand more"

James Thurber

"A woman's mind is cleaner than a man's; she changes it more often"

Oliver Herford

"I remember when the air was clean and sex was dirty"

George Burns

"I used to desire many, many things, but now I have just one desire, and that's to get rid of all my other desires"

John Cleese

"Sex is part of nature. I go along with nature"

Marilyn Monroe

"As vivacity is the gift of women, gravity is that of men"

Joseph Addison

"How are men and parking lots alike? The good ones are all taken. Free ones are mostly handicapped or extremely small"

Unknown

"I love woman. They're the best thing ever created.
If they want to be like men and come down to our level that's fine"

Mel Gibson

"Two secrets to keep your marriage brimming.
1) Whenever you're wrong, admit it. 2) Whenever you're right, shut up"

Patrick Murray

"A foolish man tells a woman to stop talking but a wise man tells her that her mouth is extremely beautiful when her lips are closed"

Robert Block

"The cruellest thing a man can do to a woman is portray her as perfection"

D.H. Lawrence

"Every girl should use what mother nature gave her before father time takes it away"

Laurence J Peter

"What a strange thing man is; and what a stranger thing woman"

Lord Byron

"I wonder why it is, that young men are always cautioned against bad girls. Anyone can handle a bad girl. It is the good girls men should be warned against"

David Niven

"The female brain is a highly intuitive emotion-processing machine, which when put to practice in the process of the society, would do much more than any man can with all his analytical perspectives"

Abhijit Naskar

"Between men and women there is no friendship possible. There is passion, enmity, worship, love, but no friendship"

Oscar Wilde

"Politics is supposed to be the second oldest profession.
I have come to realize that it is a very close resemblance to the first"

Ronald Reagan

"Behind every great man there is a surprised woman"

Maryon Pearson

"Why do people say 'grow some balls?' Balls are weak and sensitive.
If you wanna be tough, grow a vagina. Those things can take a pounding"

Betty White

"A woman may be able to change the world, but she will never be able to change a man"

Amy Snowden

"The only time a woman really succeeds in changing a man is when he is a baby"

Natalie Woods

"Men are like a deck of cards. You'll find the occasional king, but most are jacks"

Laura Swenson

"Everything in the world is about sex except sex. Sex is about power"

Oscar Wilde

"You don't have to play masculine to be a strong woman"

Mary Elizabeth Winstead

"Life is like sex. It's not always good, but it is always worth trying"

Pamela Anderson

"If men can rule the world why can't they stop wearing neckties?
How intelligent is it to start your day by tying a little noose around your neck?"

Linda Ellerbee

"Why would I make one woman miserable when I can make so many happy"

Benny Hill

"Men are like bluetooth: He is connected to you when you are nearby, but searches for other devices when you're away.

Woman are like wifi: She sees all available devices but connects to the strongest one"

Unknown

"A woman is like a tea bag – only in hot water do you realize how strong she is"

Eleanor Roosevelt

"Woman are made to be loved, not understood"

Oscar Wilde

"I would rather trust a woman's instinct than a man's reason"

Stanley Baldwin

"Sex is one of the nine reasons for reincarnation. The other eight are unimportant"

Henry Miller

"A woman's guess is much more accurate than a man's certainty"

Rudyard Kipling

"When a man sits with a pretty girl for an hour, it seems like a minute. But let him sit on a hot stove for a minute and it's longer than any hour. That's relativity"

Albert Einstein

"An intellectual is a person who's found one thing that's more interesting than sex"

Aldous Huxley

"There's no evidence whatsoever that men are more rational than women.
Both sexes are equally irrational"

Albert Ellis

"The true man wants two things: danger and play.
For that reason he wants woman, as the most dangerous plaything"

Friedrich Nietzsche

"Sex and golf are the two things you can enjoy even if you're not good at them"

Kevin Costner

"Sex is the driving force on the planet. We should embrace it, not see it as the enemy"

Hugh Hefner

"Husbands are like fires. They go out if unattended"

Zsa Zsa Gabor

"Sex is as important as eating or drinking and we ought to allow the one appetite to be as satisfied with as little restraint or false modesty as the other"

Rudyard Kipling

Lightning Source UK Ltd.
Milton Keynes UK
UKHW050959270422
402112UK00002B/62